Richard
Wentworth

D1614104

With 122 illustrations, 48 in colour

MARINA WARNER

Richard Wentworth

THAMES AND HUDSON in association with the

SERPENTINE GALLERY, LONDON

Half-title: *Range 1991*

Title page: *Third Unpronounceable Object 1989*

Published by Thames and Hudson in association with the Serpentine Gallery

British Library Cataloguing-in-Publication Data

A catalogue record for this book is available from the British Library

ISBN 0-500-27743-5

Typeset in Monophoto Baskerville
Printed and bound in Singapore

Contents

Tract (from Boost to Wham) 1993

Preface

Richard Wentworth first emerged in the late 1970s along with other British sculptors who focused on the everyday object. In their works, the waste of our industrial and consumer culture was regenerated and transformed into astute assemblages.

Wentworth's sculpture has always been marked by a preferred use of the simple, even the archetypal thing. This endows his work with a distinctly human quality. Culled primarily from the world of home and garden, his objects often hark back to ancient forms. Instantly recognizable, they extend our associations to a fund of collective memory. While rarely interfering with the objects, he manages to achieve a radical change in our perception of their ordinariness. By creating new and surprising alliances between them, Wentworth leads the viewer beyond their traditional functions to elicit unforeseen readings, involving sexuality, politics or environmental concerns. Stripped of familiarity, these objects have been metamorphosed into evocative images, into intriguing visual conundrums.

Although exuding playfulness, magic and an irreverent sense of humour, Wentworth's constructions of sensual relationships within the inanimate world are controlled by a matter-of-factness and an economy of means, which lend them their formal rigour. Human codes of behaviour – especially in their different cultural guises – frequently act as triggers for the work, which then makes patterns visible through metaphor. Chance and coincidence play important parts too, as do balance, gravity and precariousness or the often involuntary ingenuity witnessed in children's games. Equally, language is a vital source of inspiration for Wentworth, reflected in his carefully chosen titles as well as in the physical references of the work. The sculptures appear to challenge the established association of object and word: they strive to re-invent the process of naming and thus create not only new semantic possibilities but also new philosophical perspectives.

The publication of this book coincides with a major exhibition of Richard Wentworth's work at the Serpentine Gallery, London. While the exhibition brings together sculptures since 1987, the book gives a much broader and more comprehensive overview of his prolific career, illustrating works from 1981 to the present. Marina Warner's essay provides an illuminating introduction into the complexities of Wentworth's enquiry. We are grateful to her, and to Nicholas Logsdail and Susan Waxman of the Lisson Gallery, London, who have been most helpful in supplying us with the necessary information. Without the enlightened support of The Henry Moore Foundation it would not have been possible to mount the exhibition, and we are sincerely grateful for their generous financial contribution. We are also delighted that Chris Harborne, Managing Director of The Expanded Metal Company, agreed so readily to provide the artist with material free of charge to make a large installation in one of our exhibition spaces.

On behalf of the Serpentine Gallery, my warmest thanks go to the artist himself for his unfailing commitment to the exhibition, his close involvement with the selection, and especially for the great trust he has had in us. It has been a pleasure and a privilege to have collaborated with him.

Andrea Schlieker
Assistant Director
Serpentine Gallery

The house had been abandoned; its owners had moved into a new bungalow close by. Though their old home, a wooden farm in the traditional Japanese style, was virtually derelict, Richard Wentworth was fetched slippers to enter it, as if it were still lived in, cared for and should not be dirtied; it was, his hostess told him, a 'ghost house'. She was translating literally, and Wentworth was struck by the phrase, because, unlike English 'abandoned' or 'vacant', 'ghost house' suggested to him an emptiness which is full, an absence which is felt.

One of the recurring forms in Wentworth's sculpture is just such an empty house shape, and he often upturns it or tilts it or sinks it into a frame of some kind so that it offers its empty inside as the subject of the work. As a dwelling, as a home for people who may or may not be ghosts, a house is an interior; but that interior needs an exterior to exist at all. Children marking walls, roof, chimney when they draw a picture of a house encipher this spontaneously, whether or not, as Wentworth has pointed out, they live in a house that looks like that.[1] These are 'the ready-mades of the imagination'; but unlike children's versions, his leave out the windows and the door, condensing the symbol of House to its residual cave-like elements, four walls and the roof, thus tightening control of the inner space they define.

This house can be taken as culture itself – not only the domestic roof but also the shelter in which individual consciousness must live, shod as required for the purpose. *Making Do and Getting By*, the 1985 film of Richard Wentworth's photographs, plays to Ry Cooder's song 'If Walls Could Talk'. The images (p. 10), witty, low-key and affectionate, often wear for all their provisional character an air of formal poise. They show day-to-day solutions to living in the city, under the roof of culture; they record irreverent adjustments of habitat, the human flair for economical improvisation, for ingenious substitutions: cast iron railings' majestic finials become spikes for lodging lunch-break styrofoam cups after use; a child's shoe wedges the window open a crack; a pair of crossed brooms bars entrance. The 'perpetrators' have vanished, and it is their phantom traces Wentworth enjoys encountering. There's irony as well in the words on the soundtrack, for things do talk, especially to this artist, and through his perceptions, both in the subjects of his photographs and the objects in his sculpture, things speak to us, too.

The idea of trailing through the streets, chancing upon the meaningful and the marvellous, shares a great deal with André Breton's procedure in *Nadja*, the 1923 novel which turns Paris into a legible city, where love and magic and significance lie around to hand, as '*hasard objectif*' ('objective chance'), for those who have the eyes to see and respond to them and register them. Wentworth's coincidences turn up for him, too – he knows, following Picasso, that he doesn't look, but finds when others can't – but at the same time, the conjunctions in *Making Do and Getting By* aren't accidental. They were once placed, intended, made by someone, handled – however off-handedly. The off-handedness of course appeals.

His way of responding to the pattern of daily life takes the Surrealist passion for marvellous-banality to another stage of materialism, because nothing transcendental or quasi-mystical, as in Breton, brings about the processes Wentworth's photographs praise and represent: this system of signs and strategies was created by people, circulates comprehensibly among them and, with its precarious and unassuming products, makes no special claims for itself. By recording them, Wentworth brings home the value of the disregarded – but without adding a layer of pomposity, without losing lightness, without spoiling the special quality of ordinariness. The effect runs against the current perception of Surrealism, for it undermines rather than continues

[1] From a conversation with the artist, spring 1993. MW is very grateful to RW for the observations he made and help he gave from December 1992 to March 1993, and all quotations from the artist, unless otherwise noted, arose in the course of these meetings.

Photographs from *Making Do and Getting By* 1985

Surrealism's conventional love affair with weirdness. His photographs honour the mundane with minimalist restraint, they discover the latent genius in the commonplace. However, by embracing the human and social resonances struck by the object, they also evince an anthropocentric sympathy that a Sol LeWitt or a Donald Judd typically resists.

Such tenderness towards things and their placing (slippers for the ghost house) fills Wentworth's forms. Fascination with the manufactured, for the objects produced by *homo faber* has inspired a decade's work which incorporates an array of utensils, tools, vessels, furniture, both industrial and domestic, as well as a whole range of metals and fabrics. Sometimes, he uses 'raw', 'pure' materials – linen or silver – setting their elemental, pristine qualities in counterpoint to some manufactured, 'cooked' ingredient. When a natural substance, like rubber, has been vulcanized or otherwise treated, Wentworth will sometimes recall the fact of its mutation in the work's name: in *Animal, Vegetable* (1989) [p. 84], the tyre stands for the vegetable element, the house for the animal – both parts distanced from the natural by technical processes. On the whole, however, he leans towards galvanized metals, alloys, plastics, and likes to make further combinations, stretching affinities, creating unions. When he looks for the apt metaphor for these combinations, he chooses 'emulsion' – the elements bind but do not lose their distinct character. He said, in an interview in 1991, 'I live in a ready-made landscape, and I want to put it to work.'[2] He acts like Robinson Crusoe, but his desert island is the ghost house of late consumer culture, and he roams it to find what can be turned 'serviceable' again, made to make do.

Wentworth has pointed out that anthropologists assess a civilization by the number of tools it possesses; the Industrial Revolution was distinguished by the explosion of inventions: tools which made tools, or which made other things work – the spinning jenny, the turbine, the escapement. The city in which Wentworth lives, as he moves on foot or cycles between Islington and his studio in Clerkenwell, was formed by such additional, applied tooling, the prostheses of the modern human body, which have combined to make the shape of the apprehensible urban world. Wentworth resolutely resists alternative visions; his plunderings, his scavengings, his reproductions of the surrounding city's parts take numerous forms: from undisturbed retrievals in his earlier work (his brand of Duchampian ready-mades, like *Pair of Paper Bags with Large & Small Buckets*, 1982, and *Houdinium*, 1983) to the more recent emphasis on welded, cast, or assembled artefacts (*Lure, Other Dynasties, Preserve, World Soup*, 1986–91) [pp. 11, 27, 43, 56, 66, 102]. Consistent throughout has been his absorption with forms evolved over time out of practical considerations; his aesthetic stands in line with modernism's devotion to function-led simplicity.

Talking of his view of the past, he has said, 'History, I think, is probably like a pebbly beach, a complicated mass, secretively three-dimensional. It's very hard to chart what lies up against what, and why, and how deep. What does tend to get charted is what looks manageable, most recognizable (and usually linear), like the wiggly row of flotsam and jetsam, and stubborn tar deposits.'[3] The natural metaphor leads to the cultural – to the tideline of washed-up things and to tar, a substance lying like a hyphen between natural and manufactured, being the most common, available sealing substance of the container, of the boat's seams and the house's roof. (In 1981 he made a piece out of tar, *Black Puddle, White Dip* [p. 11].) The image of the tideline also reveals Wentworth's search for the uncharted arrangement; dispositions which do not strike the conventionally trained eye are not picked up by existing programmed scanning systems because they do not harmonize with what is already valued. This is a

[2] *After Modernism: The Dilemma of Influence*, dir. Michael Blackwood, 1991.

[3] Lynne Cooke, 'Making Good', in *Richard Wentworth*, exh. cat., Lisson Gallery, London, 1984, p. 11.

Black Puddle, White Dip 1981

Pair of Paper Bags with Large & Small Buckets 1982

Two Tools 1989

'Pied Beauty', *Gerard Manley Hopkins: Poems and Prose*, Harmondsworth, 1963, pp. 30–31.

key to his sculpture's often riddling character: the juxtapositions and combinations propose an alternative formal system, turning the invisible into the visible, the humdrum into the significant, ground into figure, the dumb into the telling. His buckets and ladles and ladders and water tanks and doors and strainers and ballcocks and dibbers and crutches and tins and tubs and plates and sticks are dumb things encrypted in sentences, made to talk.

Their talk is of course elusive, enigmatic, wittily mysterious. The works often seem to be teasing the viewer, making improper suggestions which ask to be quelled – and then not. The works first invite attention to the object or objects: they make their form visible, so that a rhyme sounds between a ladder and a crutch, or again, between a ladder and a strainer [p. 60]. They spring a surprise, because perception normally follows the teleology of an implement, seeing only the gaps in the strainer and not the ladder-like 'rungs' of its mesh, seeing only the downward thrust of the crutch, not the potential of ascent implied by its form. Wentworth treats the geometry of his found objects with a concentration that amounts to reverence, but he also likes to shift the emphasis from their purpose towards other possibilities: he was delighted when his younger son began using a saw with great energy – in order to produce piles of sawdust.

Topsy-turvy harvests could be merely entertaining, or cute, but Wentworth's sculpture's alterations of received meanings reach much further than that, with both disturbing and oddly satisfying results. By skewing perception of an object, he helps sharpen the sense of haecceity, of the This-ness of things, which Duns Scotus defined in the twelfth century and Gerard Manley Hopkins found such an inspiration. Hopkins looks as Wentworth does when he praises

> Landscape plotted and pieced – fold, fallow, and plough,
> And áll trádes, their gear and tackle and trim.
>
> All things counter, original, spare, strange . . .[4]

But this-ness is not allowed to rest within its own boundaries: we can admire the beckoning shiny bowl of a soup ladle, and other 'gear and tackle and trim' put to work in the sculpture, but the ladle is up to something beyond itself. And often, though we sense that it is indicating, we do not quite know what. Wentworth also likes concealment: *Cahin-Caha* (1985) or *Housey-Housey* (1986) or *Lair* (1989) [pp. 42, 96] literally throw a veil over something or hide something under the carpet; others stuff or plug or otherwise cancel the desired serviceability of shelves or chair.

Such enigma belongs to language; the objects baffle like unknown words in a foreign tongue, like a page of a foreign newspaper which contains some recognizable bits with the rest legible but incomprehensible. One of the earliest stories about language (perhaps the earliest?) uses the metaphor of building with brick and mortar, each brick a word, each course a sentence, each storey a story even, to raise the great tower of universal, mutual transparency. For the dream of the Tower of Babel is the dream of a single human language, and the wrecking God of Genesis can't accept the power it implies, and 'scatters' the builders (Gen. 11:1–9). Utopia then – one people, one language, one structure, made of baked brick – and, afterwards, here and now, nothing but Babel and babble, dissension and difference. These clashes in contemporary life tense up Wentworth's work as it leans towards utopia in its urge to restore ruins, to produce an alternative coherence, as it pays loving attention to elucidating differences in the prevailing confusion and dirt and making such differences register with due, fresh value, to set small fires burning in the pleasure

Lightweight Chair with Heavy Weights 1983

Glad That Things Don't Talk 1982

5 Anne M. Wagner, 'How Feminist Are Rosemarie Trockel's Objects?', *Parkett* 33, 1992, pp. 61–74.

6 Giovanni Anselmo, *Untitled*, 1968, in *Gravity & Grace: The Changing Condition of Sculpture 1965–1975*, exh. cat., Hayward Gallery, London, 1993, p. 53.

centres of the mind. In this respect, he stands closer to Joseph Beuys's acts of magical healing memory than to Duchamp's ironies, though the cool temperature of his work makes him the latter's closer kin.

There's a kind of hidden, pre-Babel language of things in the sculptures; indeed he has given pieces titles like *Unpronounceable Object* (1989) [*title page*]. These titles seem to offer further clues, but not solutions, in spite of their terse, precise quiddity, which lends the names themselves the air of random entries in a language vocabulary test: *Graft, Staunch, Pent, Dag, Nil By Mouth, Fable, Aqueduct* (1984–9) [pp. 58, 79]. They add a term to the riddle, but it still doesn't yield an answer like a crossword or a rebus (though there are elements of such games afoot). The works continue to tease – the pleasure of them often lies in this teasing arbitrariness, which isn't imposed or asserted, but produced gently, surreptitiously, even slyly. He says making them feels like 'walking backwards through spoken language'.

Recovering everyday tackle and gear and trim belongs in the same aesthetic as the fundamental contemporary disavowal of monumentality, of heroic carving and casting, of lofty idealist geometry – Euclidian form and Vitruvian proportion. Such sculpture offers instead formal harmonies grounded in commonplace function and fabric. Yet would it be possible to put the question, along the lines of Anne Wagner's article about Rosemarie Trockel, How masculist are Richard Wentworth's sculptures?[5] This stress on *homo faber*, this love of tools and gear, this passion for naming and this interest in sorting and applying – does it add up to a variation on the master sculptor's role? Or does it, in its rejection of heroic scale, of champion feats of forging and carving, in its domestic attachments, its reserve and unflamboyance, rather issue a statement against the tradition? Wagner argues that Trockel, far from espousing femininity with her brooms and knits, mirrors and garments, is playing with the commodities of modern life in a manner that's much more mordant and recalcitrant and polymorphous than some of her feminist partisans would claim. Through a similarly inventive, contrary-minded repertory, Wentworth avoids obvious male-bonding or even male breast-beating; his work's points of identification lead out of the gender corral, in open and conscious dissent from the Great Forefathers like David Smith and Henry Moore. He would rather claim affinity with Claes Oldenburg, especially the Oldenburg of the 'soft sculptures', the hanging drainpipes and floppy icebags; their good-tempered biomorphism acknowledges frankly and humbly the limits of human (male) aspirations. While achieving presence and scale and other traditional sculptural qualities, they still remain offbeat, modest in their inviting – embraceable – plasticity.

Oldenburg's tongue-in-cheek prods at sculpture's traditional masterfulness (its 'phallologocentricity') brings his brand of American Pop Art into close sympathy with the European postwar generation of sculptors, Italians and Germans for whom the language of the heroic body had been politicized beyond retrieval by Fascist use. Artists like Giovanni Anselmo and Mario Merz, Eva Hesse and Joseph Beuys turned to provisional and transient assemblies of hybrid elements in their contempt for the Hitlerian and Mussolinian aesthetic of portentous, classicizing, eternal anthropomorphy. Wentworth belongs in spirit to this revolt: one in which white marble can only appear with an ironical twist (a lettuce leaf for a laurel wreath).[6]

Wentworth likes objects that are called after the stuff they are made of: a rubber, a glass, a straw, a tin, a cork, a cane. He questions with his fingers the intrinsic character of materials; touch at times seems more important to him than sight. But this aesthetic should be seen in the context of a broader rejection of representation itself and representation's traditional connections with anthropomorphism and the pastoral – with dream conjurings of ideal bodies and other places. This-ness means here-and-now-ness, too, it turns its back on the sublime as well as its high and cloudy fantasies, in which a certain vision of nature has played such an important part. In 1993, Wentworth wandered through the streets of London taking more photographs – not to keep as part of his own work this time, but to show students, by 'negative example': he shot billboards advertising rum and holidays abroad, to point out how such imagery 'can change the temperature, wallpaper the world with proposals of escape which are confusing'. The flux of images in contemporary life, the scrambled messages of consumer stimuli encoded in phantom forms, in photographs and film, have accumulated to produce the affectless continuum which has been defined as the postmodern condition: 'We can beam everything up,' he says, 'even though we can't really be there – it's the difference between listening and hearing.' Wentworth opposes to this the individual presence of forms, often anchored, sometimes skied. They do not evoke by simulation: they are themselves. When the world is filled with images, art reclaims the object; when the experience is permeated with and altered by mediated pictures of a fabricated elsewhere, resistance concentrates the artist's mind on the real.

Yet the real object, Wentworth then finds, will not remain stable; even the most commonplace bucket, broom, chair or table, will conduct meanings that lie beyond appearance. Language tends to metaphor, not description; its visual representations similarly lead elsewhere. The artist also recoils, however, from the fantastic metamorphoses routinely wrought in contemporary imagery, from the canny jokiness of surreal advertising and the squashy fluid shape-shifting of Disney cartoons to the conversions and transformations of some sculptors; he seeks to expand the virtuality of the object, to keep faith with it, not to denature it or pervert it.

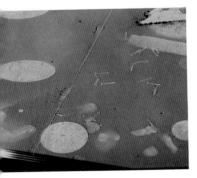

He is aware that his fidelity to implements and their integrity could seem folksy, that a nostalgia for visibly crafted objects and a lost world of universal coherence to which they once belonged might appear to inform his scavenging in house-clearance yards and his reclamation of old light bulbs, or of zinc bathtubs. But Wentworth is no throwback ruralist, or even Adorno-like artisan, renouncing capitalism's megalomania for heroic handicrafts. His allegiance to the object springs from his quixotic, affectionate relation to the world. He cites Jacques Tati, especially the Tati of *Traffic* and *Playtime*, and considers him an influence, alongside much more barbed and sombre students of the urban scene, like Brassaï. Comparing himself to a dog, he says he 'sniffs out what is essentially opaque and resistant'; he then lives with it in the extraordinary jumble of his studio as if with a lot of prize bones waiting to be dug up again and played with and savoured and put back into circulation.

Studio dust, 1992

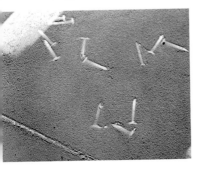

Parts of his studio, mantled in a kind of brown soot rather than dust, look like premeditated still lives – quiet, fierce statements about decrepitude and time; in other parts, as if in the prop room of an abandoned film studio, or the back yard of a junk shop, stacks of oddments, of cupboards and galoshes, bicycle wheels and coal shovels, funnels and folding tables defy all laws of category and order. But they are waiting to be assigned their roles – sometimes it happens, sometimes it doesn't. Wentworth does not know, and seldom makes *a priori* plans. 'It's as fumbling as that. I like the world revealing itself, I like aberrations, I like seeing the road dug up, I like being reminded that we're just a collection of plumbing though we can't see it.' He also sometimes talks of mudlarks – boys in the slime of the Thames, recovering debris exposed by the ebb of the tide.

But in the resulting sculptures, the pall of dust has been lifted, the mud washed away,

Surd 1991

Pablo Picasso *Still Life with Jug and Apples*
1919

⁷ *Pre-Industrial Utensils 1150–1800* (exh.
cat.), Museum Boymans-van Beuningen,
Rotterdam, 1991. Texts by A. P. E.
Ruempol and A. G. A. van Dongen.

⁸ Ian Jeffrey, 'Things, with Words', in
Richard Wentworth, exh. cat., Lisson
Gallery, London, 1986, p. 13.

the jumble lucidly sorted, and the soup of leftovers reversed back in time to basic, pristine ingredients. Though Wentworth's sculptures never look romantic, they share one thing in common with Romanticism: they partake of ruins in their character – ruins restored, consecrated, by representation as art. One of the very first things he really desired as a child – and which he managed to get – was a cast numeral identifying a tree in the school grounds which had been struck by lightning.

Yet he of course rejects any look of ruin, or of repair. Few of his works, however unaltered they appear, actually reveal their long sojourn among the studio lumber. His desire drives towards the symbol of the tree, as conveyed by its unique number, not its image.

Two principles seem to prompt his decisions to make a particular work out of his surrounding detritus and disorder: first, an aesthetic choice of forms which challenge tradition – out of the very heart of tradition; and secondly, the object's potential in a semantic code. The point of Wentworth's ladders and ladles and buckets is that while they are new, often tool-made, mass-produced, they could be very old; as shapes they have been around as long as the pyramid and the column and longer than the dome. They have, in all their humdrum and throwaway character, a claim to antiquity as legitimate as the great monuments of civilization. As such, they offer an alternative glossary of form, without the noble breeding of their more famous counterparts in the tradition of art. Curators as well as artists are becoming more sensitive to the existence of such rich formal material and exhibiting 'low' vessels in amongst 'high' art – the oil jar next to the kouros. The Boymans-van Beuningen Museum in Rotterdam has opened a wing dedicated to vernacular design – household equipment of every kind from baby bottles to vacuum cleaners.⁷ In a fine essay on Wentworth's work, written for his Lisson Gallery show in 1986, Ian Jeffrey commented, 'If [his] art is like any other art it is like that of de Hooch, a plain dealer in gutted fish, hand pumps, door latches and apple peel, as well as TIME, LIGHT, SPACE and GRAVITY.'⁸ In the domestic decorum and tenderness of the Dutch master painter of interiors, Jeffrey defiantly found sympathy with a leading exponent of Goldsmiths' College modernism – yet his suggestion is not as wayward as it may seem, for the allusion to de Hooch does highlight Wentworth's intimacy.

At the same time, the modest objects and instruments whose meanings Wentworth bends and alters belong in a sign system of his own devising which takes them into a very different realm of representation from the seventeenth-century painter. The enduringness of such forms as bottles and tubes, tubs and dishes, albeit in obscurity, fits them to function as symbols in a private language, small-scale, succinct, non-invasive, not hectoring, intensely felt. The artist doesn't make many visual puns in the manner of Picasso's famous *Still Life with Jug and Apples* of 1919, though *Cumulus* (1991) [p. 109], showing a ladder ascending to a glass shelf of white plates, rhymes on ascension and heaven with a similar light mimicry and economy of means. Generally, Wentworth's works play with linguistics' building blocks of signifier and signified, and leave aside anthropomorphic resemblance.

He used to incline to pairing – a torch lain on one crisp white pillow, a cold chisel on another beside it (*Early Hours*, 1982 [p. 22]), or a rock and a paper bag side by side (*Domino*, 1984 [p. 36]); these encounters can suggest couplings, with a hint at absurdity and clumsiness, but sometimes they level with politics, too. *Unmatched Pair (Jerusalem)* (1986 [p. 50]) consists of two buckets, welded at their lips where they touch, apparently identical and equally full – but one reaches the height of the other only because it is raised on a yellow cloth; *Fable* (1988 [p. 79]) – a shiny bowl set high

ain 1992

_etter to MW, January 1993.

up, out of reach, contents out of sight, from a tall ladder set askew – hints at a different cryptic story of frustration and longing. Since the late 1980s, the sculptor has been combining three or more elements rather more frequently, gradually moving into assemblies of plural and repeated forms – *World Soup* (1991 [p. 102]), with its several buried tins of pet food; *Stile* (1991 [p. 99]), with its array of brooms and brushes piercing an office desk. Juxtaposing familiar and dissimilar objects gives birth to other presences, ghosts, beyond visibility.

Wentworth explores weights and measures and gauges and their various systems of notation in order to give meaning to his objects. The terms of measurement appeal, like another language, for they're necessarily encoded (it's been a while since the Emperor of China weighed an elephant by first loading the animal onto a barge, marking the waterline, unloading the elephant, piling stones on to the barge until it had sunk to the same level, and then weighing the stones one by one). One series of sculptures uses the large, childish faces of dials on scales, in conjunction with light bulbs: there's a contradiction there, pointing to the limits of this particular measuring system, for one element – light – won't register in the same way as another, earth or water, which would tip the scales. He's also referred in various works to Mercator's projection, to Fahrenheit's code for temperature, and has included globes and tape measures and rulers in others [pp. 91, 30]; in *Some History* (1991 [p. 95]), for instance, one of his empty houses suggests the fullness of its past – and present – as it sits upside down in an old filing cabinet hoisted on the wall and hollow like a silo, against the kind of marked off measurements that archaeologists make in a dig.

These ways of measuring substitute one sayable term for something unsayable. They provide an answer to the conundrums, How to communicate phenomena, how to speak of heat or cold? How to map flat the curving world – in short, how to turn the ungraspable into the coherent?

Incoherence tantalizes him – he wants to touch bottom in it, because, if he can, it will cease to be incoherent. In a letter, he wrote: 'I looked more closely at the stand of Made-in-China paraphernalia in my newsagent's – notes from the Bank of Toy, plastic coins, fighter planes, dinosaurs, toy guitars, Diana dress-up dolls, Wild West figures, wild animals, doctor's sets – extraordinary for their cultural mixtures, gender divisions, scale jumps and modesty. Old-fashioned, one might say, a basic repertoire of playthings which will run and run. I haven't done anything with this probably because they're already ciphers, at one remove from the real thing. Knowing where they're made makes them even stranger. I really wonder what these things can possibly mean to the person charged with making them. They have this in common with lots of other manufactured things – "authentic baseball" hats which say inside "Made in Bangladesh" – before they move through the retailing value-added sieve.'[9]

Just as any child can learn a language which will tie grown-ups' tongues in knots and break their brains – Chinese or Xhosa for example – Wentworth thinks himself in the position of such a stranger, sorting the confusion, finding rhyme and reason in the incoherent. Just as any child can deploy a symbolic world in the microcosm of a game – a pocket mirror for a pond, a twig for a tree, some leaves for dishes and grass for food, and the dolls are having a picnic out in the country – he plays at assigning meanings to those things that are 'counter, original, spare, strange'. 'Pretend' is one of Richard Wentworth's words, and he uses it as a noun, as it were 'art' or 'sculpture' or a way of being: 'Do you think animals have pretend?' he once asked his children. Part of pretend is assigning names to things, arbitrarily, as part of the game's internal rules. Labelling preoccupies him – it's a gesture against incoherence, but in so many aspects

Joe and Felix Wentworth, 1992

Hurricane 1987

Chinese ideogram *Hé*

[10] Ian Buruma, 'Japanese Avant-Garde', in *A Cabinet of Signs: Contemporary Art from Post-Modern Japan*, exh. cat., Tate Gallery Liverpool, and Whitechapel Gallery, London, 1991, p. 17.

MW thanks Irène Andreae and Barney Wan for their help.

of contemporary fabrication, it only aggravates the condition. Especially in Japan, the quintessential postmodern country, where he noted that 'when a garment or a product doesn't have a brand name, it can be called *sabishii* – which means "deprived".' In order to belong to the Western cultural order, English is used there as a code – words with no referents, as in the slogan, 'Let's go sports for the spirit city!'[10]

Richard Wentworth is repelled and attracted by this non-sense, because it is meaninglessness at its most mind-numbing as well as play at its most pure.

Many of the old words for playing, or for games, are the same as the words for joking, and they're related to juggling, too, as in Latin *iocare*, or Old French *jongler*. Juggling was the art of the *jongleur*, the travelling tumbler and acrobat who also told stories and sang songs and entertained audiences with jokes, like the stand-up comedians of today. Wentworth's 'pretend' juggles words and things, stories and presences, using sleight of hand to put small and ordinary objects in the place of larger concepts (his line of flags – steel chairs on the roof at crazy angles – for the 1992 show in Copenhagen was an inspired variation [p. 112]). He brings experience down to earth, like children playing on the floor, but keeps its mysteries, too, like the same children, who know in their heads exactly what is going on and are impatient with newcomers to the game. There's nothing like a secret language for enticing someone on the outside in.

Children everywhere build towers of bricks; such play is a sign of a human, solemnly tested by paediatricians. Richard Wentworth's last Christmas card showed his sons proudly sitting on a pile of bricks – real ones, from a wall they had demolished. Here 'pretend' mixes to 'for-real', as it sometimes can do, to odd, exciting effect. He likes passing back and forth through the categories of play and action, simulation and reality, making light of gravity with tilted and tipped and skied pieces, just like one of the acrobats or jugglers whose photographs he collects and pins on the studio wall.

His work can be laconically funny, showing a dry wit, throwing in toys playfully, as in the early Babar and Celeste series made of transfigured dog dishes [p. 20], or the office chairs threaded with a pair of hanging balls (*Lightweight Chair with Heavy Weights*, 1983 [p. 12], *Siege*, 1984 [p. 25]), or, in *Neighbour, Neighbour* (1988 [p. 81]), where two of his signature houses, suspended in mid-air, are screwed up together with a single layer of insulating felt squeezed tight between their adjoining walls. Sometimes his cunning permutations strike a much darker note, even while they still wear the strolling player's insouciant air: in *Hurricane* (1987), a wire basket of old light bulbs is plugged with a thick, solid slug of concrete, lying menacingly close to the level of the bulbs – a conflict of textures, thin against thick, fragile against impervious, conveying with deft metonymy the destructiveness of the freak storm that year. Similar materials, but with added bulbs and a thinner crust, evoke the catastrophe of Chernobyl in *Preserve* (1987–8 [p. 66]) – the concrete entombment of the radioactive wasteland.

Analysing Wentworth's works sometimes seems tantamount to betraying their qualities of allusiveness and tact, to manhandling them to make them shake out their secrets. It may be apt, in this context, that the Chinese ideogram that most resembles a child's drawing of a house – *Hé* – does not carry a primary meaning of 'dwelling', but signifies 'closed' or 'shut', and as a verb means 'join' or 'combine'. This ancient cipher of a shut house symbolizes combining and joining – the fundamental processes of Wentworth's sculpture, the building blocks of his art. His work combines elements to propose an alternative, private, invented ideographic language, using domesticated, common things which somehow retain their secrets – and it compels in the same way as a closed door, exciting curiosity, invites entry, as an empty house still stirs.

Impedimenta 1

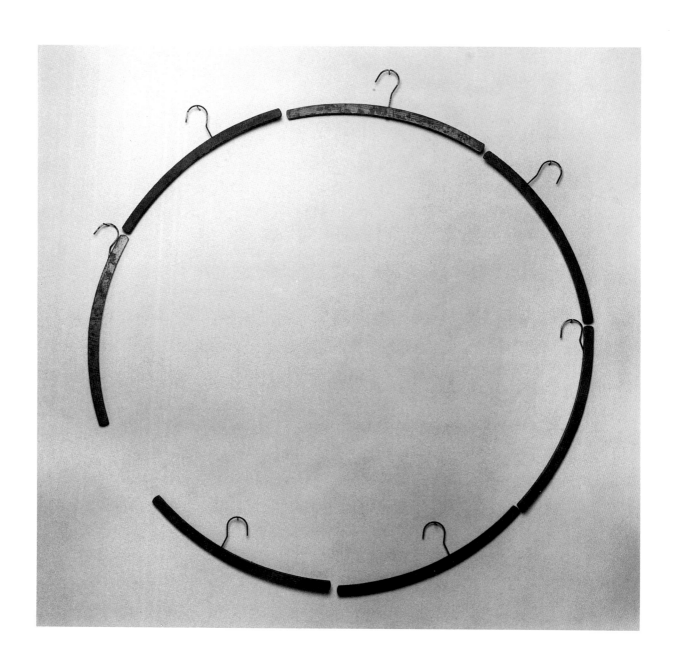

Idiot Circle 1981

Man and Boy 1982

Babar and Fido 1982

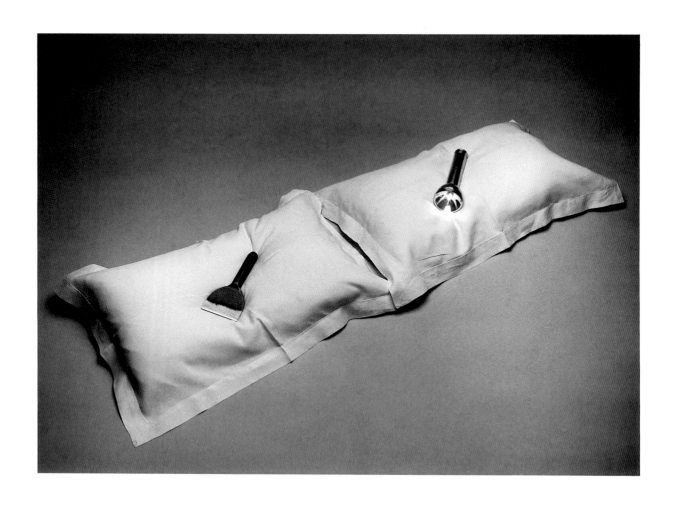

Early Hours 1982

Dry Crying 1982

Heist (for S.E.) 1983

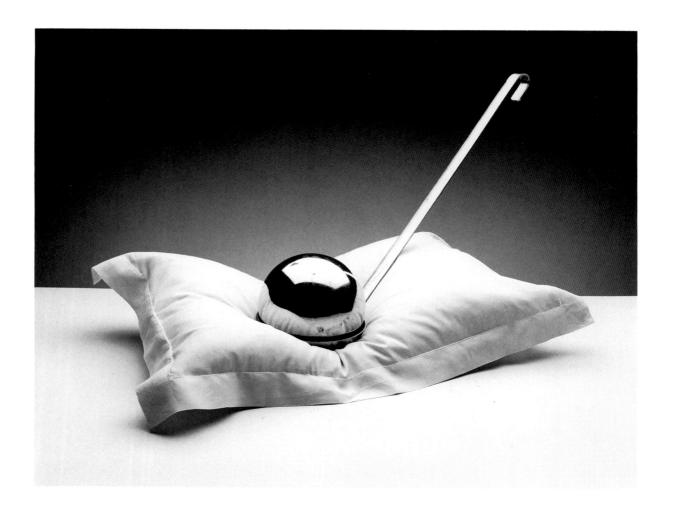

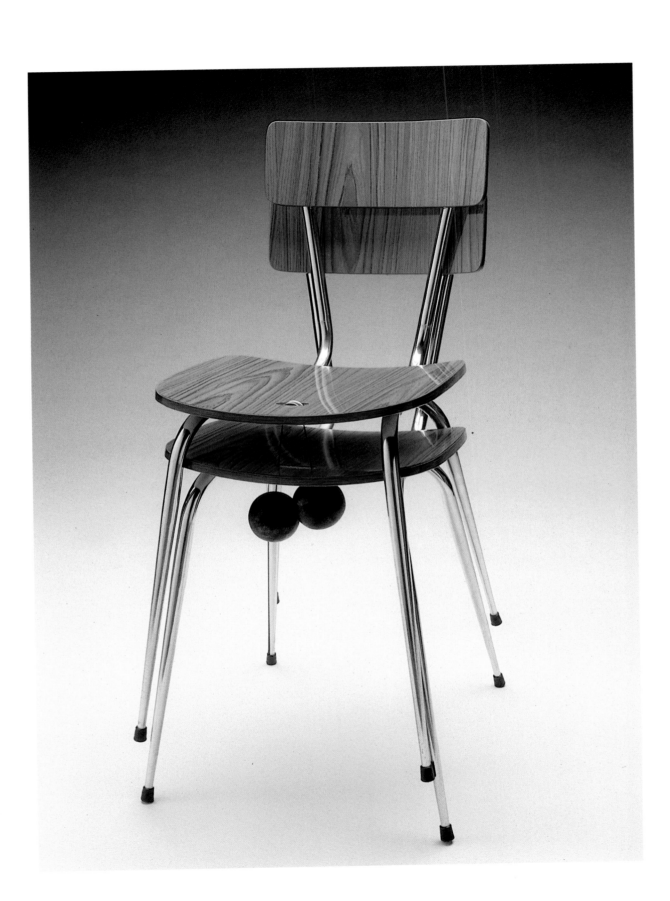

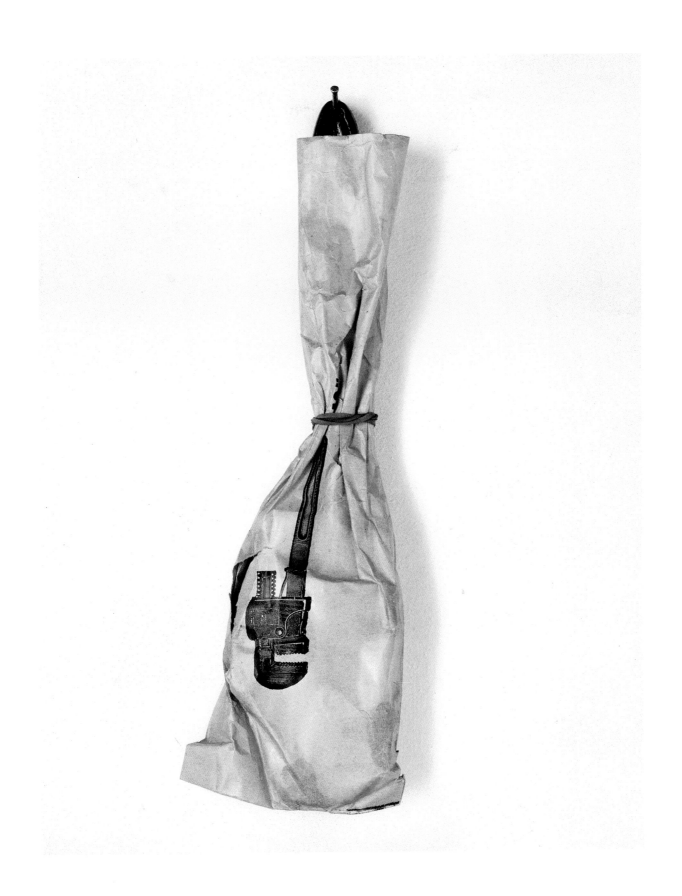

Bench 1984

Antarctica with Lead Balls 1984

nde 1984   *Eleven Month Dusk* 1983

Toy 1983

Saving Daylight 1984

Place 1984

Pyre 1984

Yellow Eight 1985

Profit and Loss 1985

Gosse 1984

Cahin-Caha 1985

Lure 1986

Siphon 1984–85

Pétard 1984

Logo 1986

Shrink 1985

Chinese Wall 1986

Unmatched Pair (Jerusalem) 1986

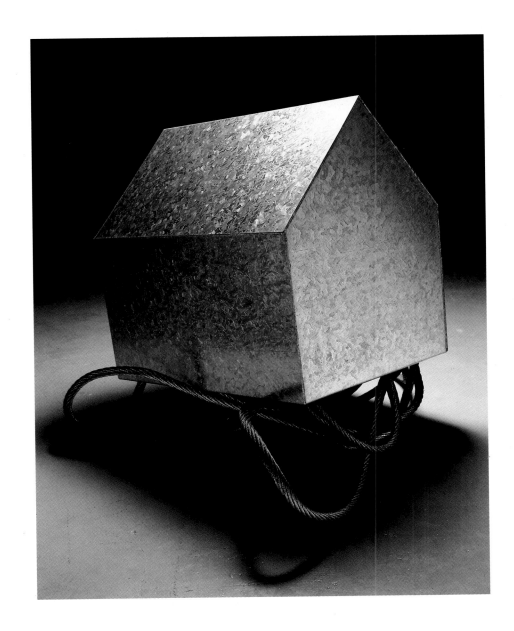

Store 1986

Shower 1984

Walking Stick 1987

Other Dynasties 1986

Year Ending 1986

Trap 1986

Spy 1986

Prairie 1987

Scope 1987

Preserve 1987–88

Taste 1

Small Thrall 1988

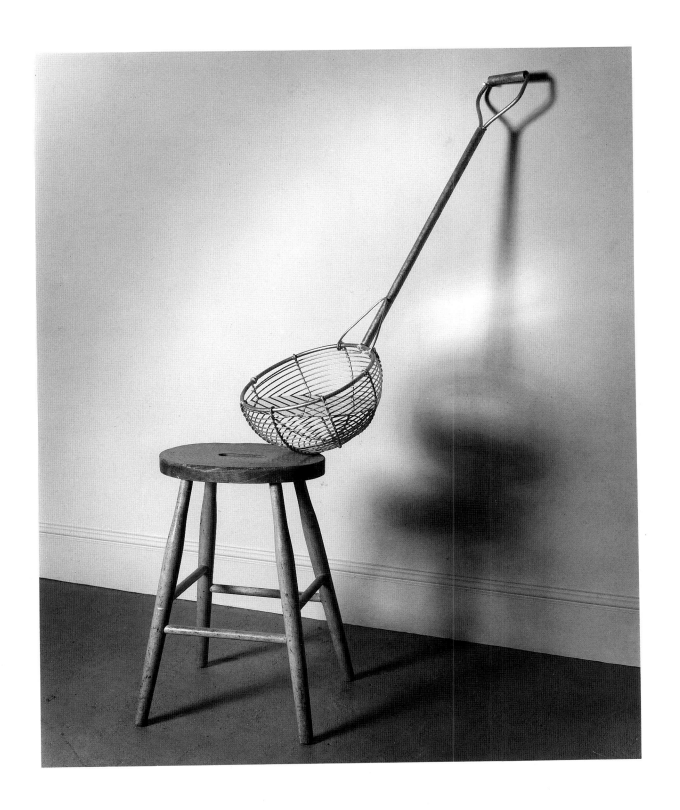

Atlas 1988

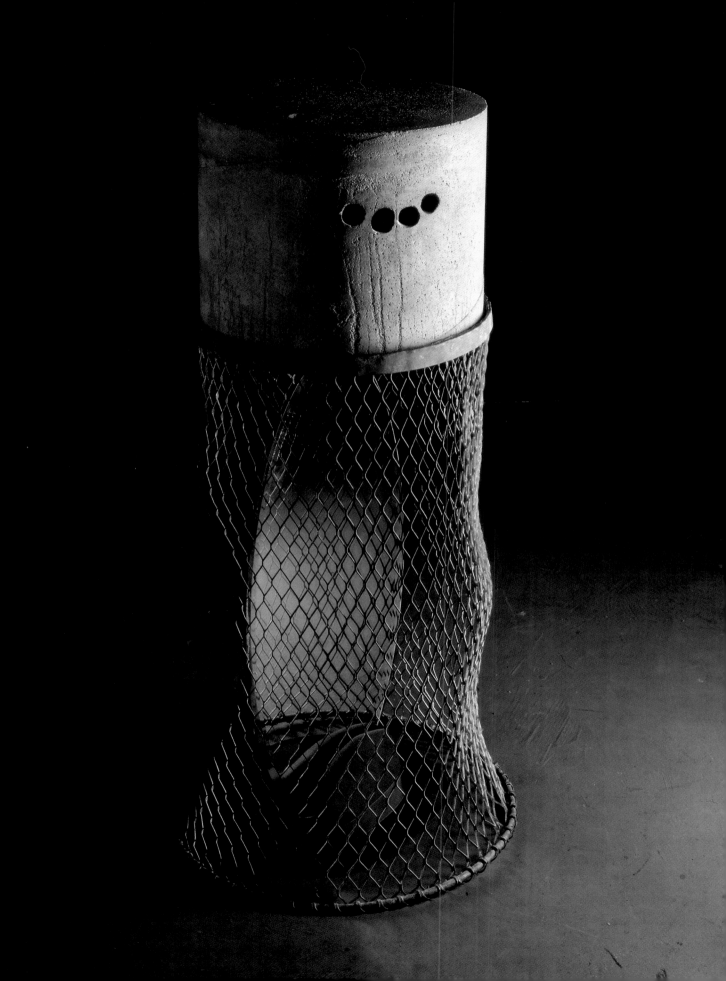

Other Geologies 1988

Small Farm 1988

Stolen Thunder 1988 (and detail)

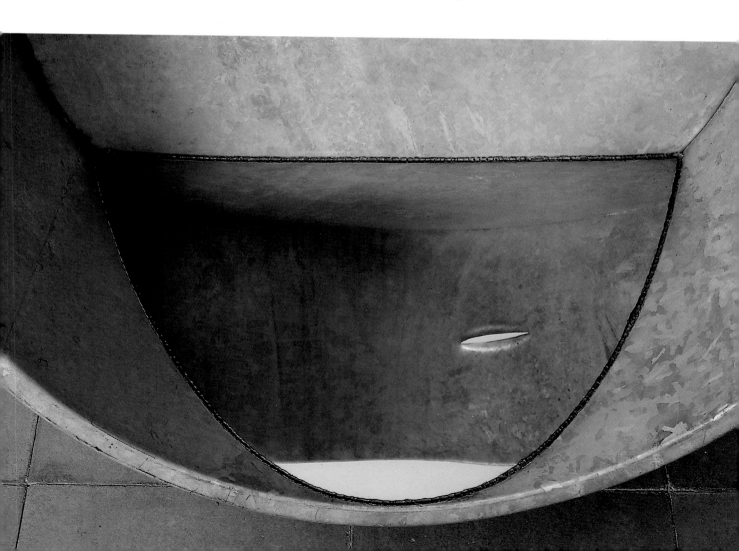

eel 1987

Ménage 1987

Little Minds 1989

English Sandwich 1988

Raft 1989

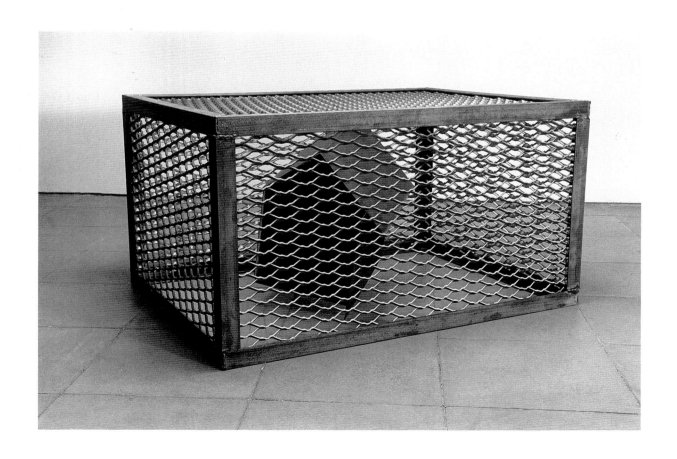

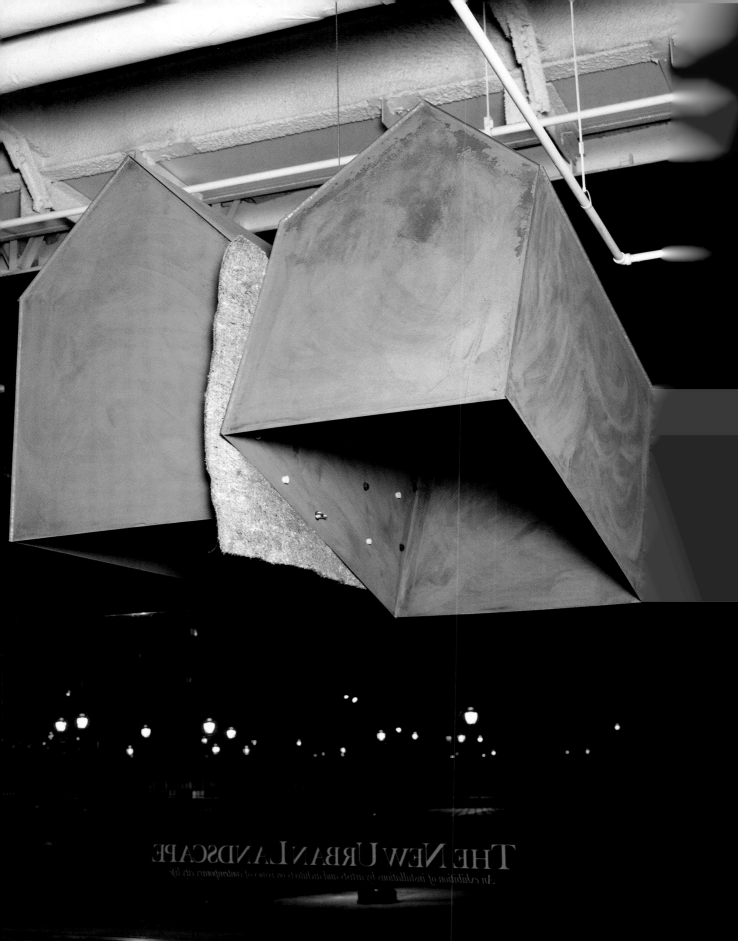

The Appian Way 1989

Odd Reds 1989

Tide *1990*

This Boy, That Boy 1987

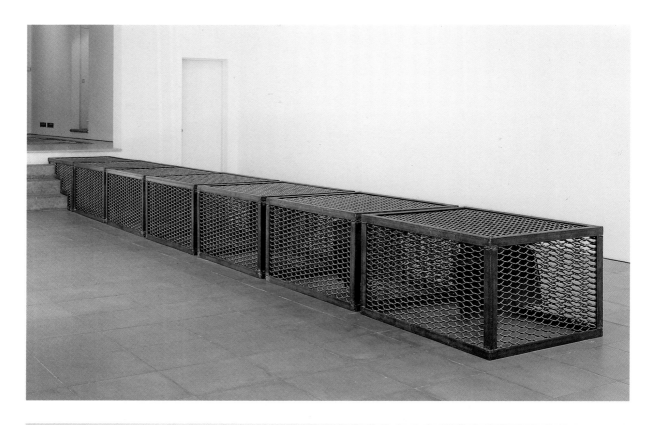

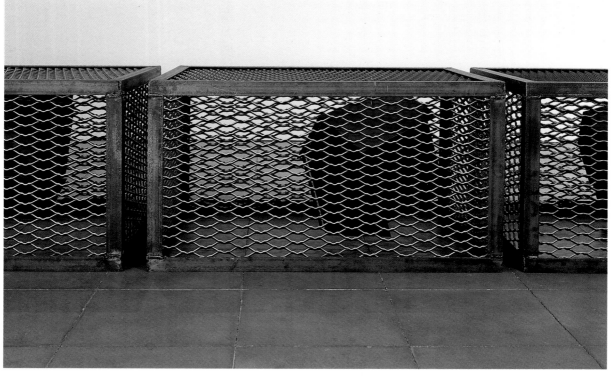

Pier 1989 (and detail)

Between 8 & 9 1989

Forebear 1 1990

Mercator 1990

Morsel and Vista 1989

Buttress 1990

Mould 1991

Some History 1991

Lair 1989

Gran Falda 1990

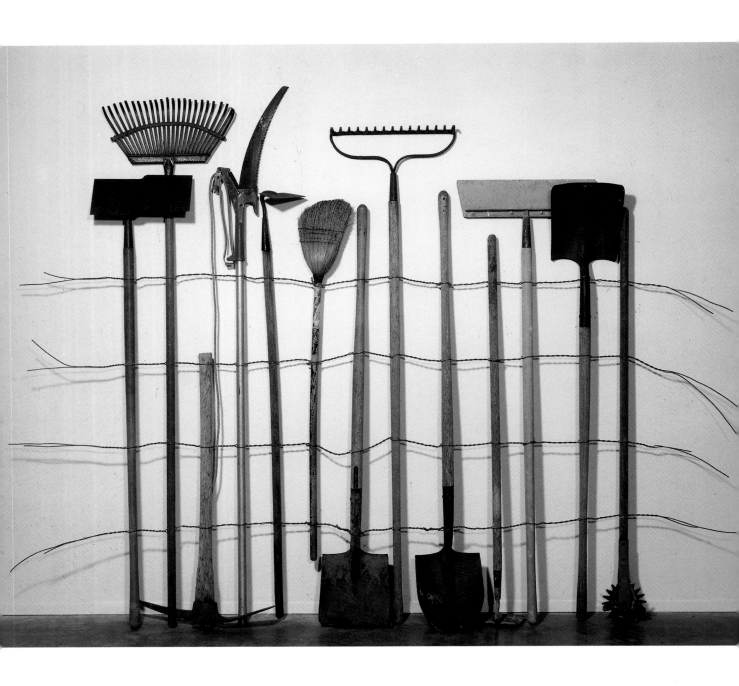

Piece of Fence 1990

Stile 1991

World Soup 1991

Island *1991*

Balcone 1991

Lips and Fingertips (for Simon Rodia) 1992

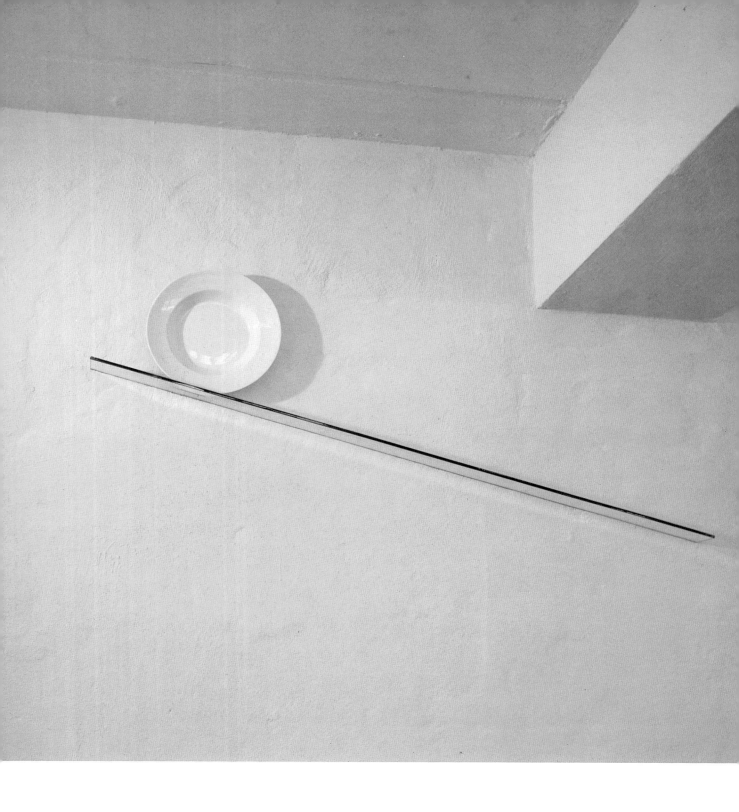

Stonehenge 1992

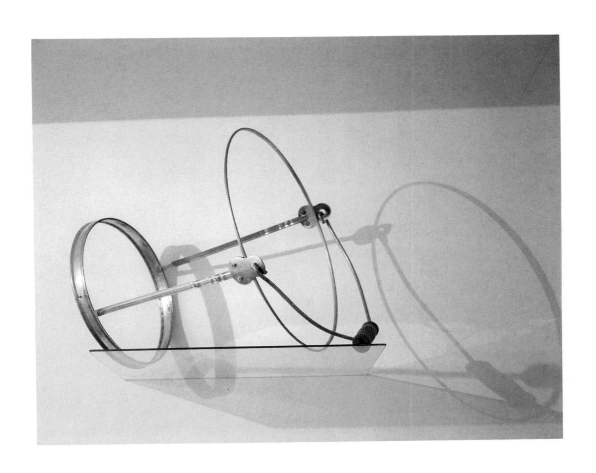

Stencil (Katagami) 1992

Twenty-Four Hour Flag 1992 (detail)

Chronology

List of Illustrations

Exhibitions

Selected Bibliography

Chronology

RICHARD WENTWORTH was born in Samoa in 1947. Based in London, he attended Hornsey College of Art from 1965 and worked with Henry Moore in 1967. From the Royal College of Art he gained an MA in 1970 and went on to teach at Goldsmiths' College, University of London, from 1971 to 1987. In 1975 and in 1978 he worked in New York. He was appointed by the prestigious German Academic Exchange Programme (DAAD) to work in Berlin from 1993 to 1994.

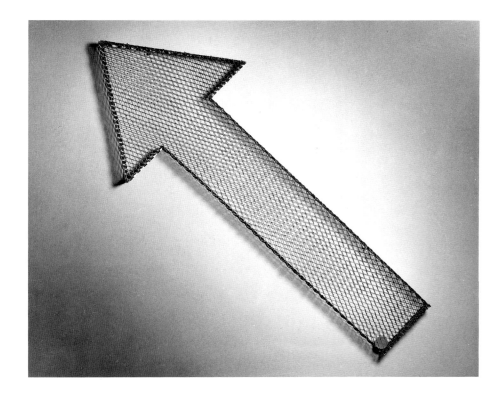

There 1989

List of Illustrations

All measurements are in centimetres

21 *35° 9′ 32° 18′* 1985
Steel and cable
405 × 72 × 120
Private collection, London

22 *Early Hours* 1982
Linen, duckdown, steel, glass
11 × 160 × 57
Courtesy Lisson Gallery London

23 *Dry Crying* 1982
Galvanized steel, cotton, cork,
light bulb
31 × 35 × 35
Private collection, London

24 *Heist (for S.E.)* 1983
Linen, duckdown, gilded lead,
tinned steel
60 × 90 × 65
Saatchi Collection, London

25 *Siege* 1984
Laminated wood, steel, brass,
lead, cable
86 × 41 × 44
Private collection, London

26 *The Marriage of Babar and Celeste*
1983
Linen, duckdown, gilded
aluminium
62 × 91 × 66
Private collection, London

27 *Houdinium (Large Resale Version)*
1983
Forged steel, printed paper, rubber
40 × 12 × 4
Courtesy Lisson Gallery London

28 *Bench* 1984
Wood, laminated plywood, lead,
steel, plastic
85 × 80 × 59
Courtesy Lisson Gallery London

29 *Antarctica with Lead Balls* 1984
Enamelled steel, polythene, lead
66 × 66 × 32
Courtesy Lisson Gallery London

30 *Monde* 1984
Cable and globe
47 × 50 × 50
Private collection, London

31 *Eleven Month Dusk* 1983
(photographed at 8 months)
String bag and dud light bulbs
58 × 33 × 35
Collection of the artist

32 *Toy* 1983
Galvanized and tinned steel
60 × 40 × 40
Arts Council of Great Britain,
London

33 *Queue* 1984
Steel and plastic
92 × 540 × 90
Courtesy Lisson Gallery London

34 *Saving Daylight* 1984
Tinned steel and dud light bulbs
46 × 31 × 31
Collection of the artist

35 *Place* 1984
Canvas, steel, lead, cable
85 × 39 × 45
Courtesy Lisson Gallery London

36 *Domino* 1984
Granite and paper
60 × 50 × 37
Courtesy Lisson Gallery London

37 *Pyre* 1984
Brass and rubber
40 × 34 × 33
Private collection, New York

38 *Yellow Eight* 1985
Galvanized steel and brass
32 × 62 × 31
Saatchi Collection, London

39 *Profit and Loss* 1985
Galvanized steel and brass
46 × 92 × 61
Private collection, London

40 *Gosse* 1984
Galvanized steel, aluminium, cable
28 × 66 × 48
Private collection, London

41 *Vinegar & Brown Paper* 1984
Fibreboard, paper, sisal, sealing
wax, glass

21 diameter
Collection of the artist

42 *Cahin-Caha* 1985
Wood, steel, linen, concrete
107 × 245 × 214
Courtesy Lisson Gallery London

43 *Lure* 1986 (rear view)
Steel, zinc, looking-glass, fine
sponge
77.5 × 52 × 39
Courtesy Lisson Gallery London

44 *Siphon* 1984–85
Galvanized steel and fine
sponges
92 × 92 × 11
Saatchi Collection, London

45 *Pétard* 1984
Rubber, steel, lead, cable
71 × 71 × 16
Private collection, USA

46 *Logo* 1986
Concrete, steel, rubber
38 × 41 × 36
Private collection, London

47 *Cave* 1986
Steel, canvas, leaded steel
140 × 65 × 109
Courtesy Lisson Gallery London

48 *Shrink* 1985
Galvanized steel and brass
46 × 137 × 92
Private collection, New York

49 *Chinese Wall* 1986
Galvanized steel
27.6 × 336 × 31
Courtesy Lisson Gallery London

50 *Unmatched Pair (Jerusalem)* 1986
Galvanized steel and linen
46 × 61 × 39
Courtesy Lisson Gallery London

51 *House and Home* 1986
Steel cable, wood, galvanized
steel
85 × 58 × 8
Private collection, Basel

52 *Store* 1986
Galvanized steel, paper, glass,
cord
107 × 61 × 46
Centro Cultural de Arte
Contemporaneo, Mexico

53 *Shower* 1984
Laminated wood, brass, steel,
aluminium
89 × 110 × 88
Tate Gallery, London

54 *Counting House* 1987
Leaded steel, steel, brass
140 × 65 × 109
Saatchi Collection, London

55 *Walking Stick* 1987
Wood and glass
85 × 43 × 7 and 86 × 10
Private collection, London

56 *Other Dynasties* 1986
Concrete, steel, postcards
46 × 46 × 46
Courtesy Lisson Gallery London

57 *Year Ending* 1986
Steel and concrete
74 × 46 × 46
Private collection, London

58 *Nil By Mouth* 1986
Galvanized steel, glass,
silver-plate
93 × 54 × 59
Private collection, New York

59 *Trap* 1986
Zinc
25 × 45 × 22
Private collection, London

60 *Algebra* 1986–87
Wood, rubber, vinyl
335 × 150 × 50
Saatchi Collection, London

61 *Spy* 1986
Aluminium
40 × 51 × 31
Private collection, Amsterdam

62 *Guide* 1984–88
Rubber and concrete
42 × 33 × 12
Arts Council of Great Britain,
London

63 *Prairie* 1987
Leaded steel and cable
100 × 90 × 72
Saatchi Collection, London

64 *Pair of Caves* 1987
Leaded steel, steel, canvas
141.5 × 124 × 111
Courtesy Lisson Gallery London

65 *Scope* 1987
Galvanized steel and copper
47 × 47 × 34
Private collection, London

66 *Preserve* 1987–88
Steel, concrete, dud light bulbs
35 × 44 diameter
Private collection, New York

67 *Taste* 1987
Concrete, expanded steel, felt,
looking-glass
94.5 × 48
Courtesy Lisson Gallery London

68 *Small Thrall* 1988
Wood, steel, brass, cord
37 × 38 × 56, 23.5 × 18.5 × 24,
37.5 × 1 diameter
Courtesy Lisson Gallery London

69 *Atlas* 1988
Wood, galvanized steel, brass
137 × 29.5 × 23.5
Private collection, La Jolla, CA

70 *Clasp* 1988
Galvanized steel, brass, cable
40 × 27 × 109
Private collection, USA

71 *Thinks . . .* 1987
Steel, concrete, felt, looking-glass
103 × 49 diameter
Private collection, Atlanta, GA

72 *Other Geologies* 1988
Galvanized steel

100 × 35 × 30
Private collection, La Jolla, CA

73 *Small Farm* 1988
Steel and steel wool
29 × 45 × 46
Courtesy Lisson Gallery London

74 *Stolen Thunder* 1988 (and detail)
Galvanized steel and brass
140 diameter × 54
Courtesy Lisson Gallery London

75 *eel* 1987
Galvanized steel
35 × 245 × 100
Private collection, La Jolla, CA

76 *Ménage* 1987
Galvanized steel
40 × 235 × 235
Courtesy Lisson Gallery London

77 *Little Minds* 1989
Concrete, wood, galvanized
steel, brass
110 × 71 × 72
Private collection, London

78 *English Sandwich* 1988
Glass, wood, felt, looking-glass
60 × 40 × 30
Courtesy Lisson Gallery London

79 *Fable* 1988
Stainless steel, brass, cable, wood
18 × 48 diameter and
389 × 36 × 8
Courtesy Lisson Gallery London

80 *Raft* 1989
Expanded steel, steel, cable
65.5 × 180 × 87.5
Courtesy Lisson Gallery London

81 *Neighbour, Neighbour* 1988
Steel, felt, cork, cable
107 × 153 × 122
Courtesy Lisson Gallery London

82 *The Appian Way* 1989
Painted and rusted steel and
rubber
48 × 114 × 95 and 52 × 112 × 97
Courtesy Lisson Gallery London

83 *When in Rome* 1989
Steel and rubber
278 × 193
Courtesy Lisson Gallery London

84 *Animal, Vegetable* 1989
Steel, rubber, granite
164 × 147 × 71
Courtesy Lisson Gallery London

85 *Odd Reds* 1989
Steel
79 × 31.5 × 87.5
Private collection, New York

86 *Tide* 1990
Painted steel
91.5 × 91.5 × 30.5
Private collection, Italy

87 *This Boy, That Boy* 1987
Leaded and galvanized steel and
brass
64 × 36 × 155
Private collection, London

88 *Pier* 1989 (and detail)
Expanded steel, steel, cable
65.5 × 875 × 88
Courtesy Lisson Gallery London

89 *Between 8 & 9* 1989
Steel
282 × 100 × 45.5
Courtesy Lisson Gallery London

90 *Forebear 1* 1990
Steel
78.7 × 115.5 × 94
Courtesy Lisson Gallery London

91 *Mercator* 1990
Galvanized steel and steel
400 × 400 × 150 overall
Courtesy Lisson Gallery London

92 *Morsel and Vista* 1989
Steel
Overall 71.5 × 350 × 182
Courtesy Lisson Gallery London

93 *Buttress* 1990
Wood, aluminium, brick
57 × 73.6 × 10
Private collection, USA

94 *Mould* 1991
Tinned and galvanized
expanded steel
28 × 25 × 19
Private collection, Turin

95 *Some History* 1991
Painted and galvanized steel
93 × 45 × 33
Courtesy Lisson Gallery London

96 *Lair* 1989
Steel and carpet
36.5 × 300 × 385
Courtesy Lisson Gallery London

97 *Gran Falda* 1990
Aluminium and wire mesh
411.5 × 167.6 × 182.8
Courtesy Lisson Gallery London

98 *Piece of Fence* 1990
Tools and wire
181.6 × 228.6 × 15.2
Private collection, USA

99 *Stile* 1991
Steel, linoleum, brooms
155 × 141 × 77
Courtesy Lisson Gallery London

100 *Aide Mémoire* 1991
Galvanized steel, galvanized
steel painted with brass, plastic
51.5 × 56 × 32
Courtesy Lisson Gallery London

101 *Darktime* 1990
Galvanized steel
28 × 76.2 × 43.2
Private collection, USA

102 *World Soup* 1991
Galvanized steel and tin
11.5 × 74 × 71.5
Private collection, Switzerland

103 *Man and the Animals #2* 1991
Galvanized steel and tin
26 × 26.5 × 15.2
Courtesy Lisson Gallery London

104 *Lapse* 1991
Stainless and sprung steel and
steel

$35 \times 49 \times 26$
Courtesy Lisson Gallery London

105 *Flung* 1991
Painted steel
$52 \times 51 \times 58$
Courtesy Lisson Gallery London

106 *Husk* 1992
Galvanized and stainless steel
$60 \times 49 \times 68$
Courtesy Lisson Gallery London

107 *Island* 1991
Galvanized and painted steel
$6 \times 33 \times 31$
Courtesy Lisson Gallery London

108 *Balcone* 1991
Painted steel, linoleum and tools
$205 \times 157 \times 78$
Courtesy Lisson Gallery London

109 *Cumulus* 1991
Wood, glass, ceramic
$320 \times 90 \times 23$
Courtesy Lisson Gallery London

110 *Friday* 1992
Cement footprint in concrete
floor
Dimensions variable
Installation, TAPKO,
Copenhagen
Courtesy Lisson Gallery London

111 *Lips and Fingertips (for Simon Rodia)* 1992
Glass and ceramic
$35 \times 1100 \times 38$
Courtesy Lisson Gallery London

112 *Stonehenge* 1992
Glass and porcelain
$28 \times 135 \times 12.5$
Installation, TAPKO,
Copenhagen
Courtesy Lisson Gallery London

113 *Stencil (Katagami)* 1992
Glass, galvanized steel, wood
$32 \times 43.3 \times 37$ and $42 \times 76 \times 37$
with shadow
Courtesy Lisson Gallery London

114 *Twenty-Four Hour Flag* 1992
(detail)
Steel and laminate
Dimensions variable
Installation, TAPKO,
Copenhagen
Courtesy Lisson Gallery London

116 *There* 1989
Galvanized steel and glass
$73 \times 76 \times 6$
Private collection, London

(back cover)
Meal 1990
Cast iron
120, 70, 90 and 60
'Festival Landmarks '90', Gateshead

Photographs, by page number: Jon Abbott 81; Peter Cox, Amsterdam 16 middle; Ant Crichfield, London 11 below, 55, 72, 74, 80, 84, 88, 92, 96; Jens Honig, Copenhagen 110, 112; Giorgio Mussa, Turin 108; Sue Ormerod, London 103; Mike Parsons, London, printed by Keith Taylor *half-title*, 11 above, 12 above, below, 14 above, 18–20, 22–4, 26–8, 30, 31, 33–40, 42–50, 52–4, 56–9, 68, 69, 73, 77, 87, 93, 100, 102, 104, 107, 116; Andrew Putler 17, 21, 65; John Riddy, London 6, 106; Stephen White, London 15, 109; Gareth Winters, London 75, 78, 82, 83, 91, 105; Damien Wootten *back cover*

	'Object Lessons', The Banff Centre Walter Phillips Gallery, Banff, Alberta
	'Britannia: British Art of the 80's', Liljevalchs Konstall Stockholm and Sara Hilden Art Museum, Tampere, Finland
1988	'Redefining the Object', Wright State University Gallery, Dayton, Ohio, and tour
	'Starlit Waters: British Sculpture – an International Art, 1968–86', Tate Gallery, Liverpool
	'Britannica: 30 Years of Sculpture', Musée des Beaux-Arts André Malraux, Le Havre, and tour
	'New Urban Landscape', World Financial Center, New York
	Galerie Monica Spruth, Cologne
1989	'British Sculpture, 1960–1988', Museum van Hedendaagse Kunst, Antwerp
	'Another Focus: Photographs by Painters and Sculptors', Karsten Schubert, London
	'Richard Wentworth, Grenville Davey, Gerard Williams', Sala 1, Rome
1990	'Biennale of Sydney', Sydney
	'Glasgow's Great British Art Exhibition', McLellan Galleries, Glasgow
	'The New Urban Landscape', World Financial Center, New York
	'Now for the Future', Arts Council of Great Britain, Hayward Gallery, London
1991	'Kunst Europa', Karlsruhe Kunstverein
	'The Kitchen Show', St Gallen, Switzerland
	'Objects for the Ideal Home: The Legacy of Pop Art', Serpentine Gallery
1992	'Oh! cet écho!', Centre culturel suisse, Paris
	'Process to Presence', Locks Gallery, Philadelphia
1992–93	'The Saatchi Gift', Tate Gallery, London
1993	'British Sculpture from the Arts Council Collection', Arts Council of Great Britain, Derby Museum and Art Gallery, and tour

elected Bibliography

1987   Paul Bonaventura, 'Today, We Have Naming of Parts', *Artefactum*, September–October, pp. 30–35.

1992   Kiyoshi Kusumi, 'Compacted Impact, an interview with Richard Wentworth', *Bijitsu Techno*, May, pp. 144–53.
James Roberts, 'Speaking in Tongues', *Frieze*, 3, pp. 24–7.
Jonathan Watkins, 'Lighting Fires, Richard Wentworth interviewed by Jonathan Watkins', *Frieze*, 3, pp. 28–31.

Books and Exhibition Catalogues

1981   Fenella Crichton, 'Symbols, Presences and Poetry', in *British Sculpture in the Twentieth Century* (exh. cat.), Whitechapel Art Gallery, London.

1983   Fenella Crichton, 'When Form engenders Attitude', in *The Sculpture Show* (exh. cat.), Hayward Gallery, London, Arts Council of Great Britain.

1984   *Richard Wentworth* (exh. cat.), Lisson Gallery, London. Text by Lynne Cooke and interview by Stuart Morgan.
Richard Wentworth, *Making Do and Getting By*, Tate Gallery, London.
Richard Francis, 'Richard Wentworth's etymology' in *The British Show* (exh. cat.), British Council, Australia.

1985   *Making Do and Getting By* (exh. cat.), Whitechapel Art Gallery, London.
Richard Francis, *The Poetic Object* (exh. cat.), Douglas Hyde Gallery, Dublin.

1986   Ian Jeffrey, 'Things, with Words', in *Richard Wentworth* (exh. cat.), Lisson Gallery, London.

1987   Lynne Cooke, 'Between Image and Object: The "New British Sculpture"', *A Quiet Revolution: British Sculpture since 1965* (exh. cat.), Museum of Contemporary Art, Chicago, San Francisco Museum of Modern Art, and Thames and Hudson, London and New York.
Inscriptions and Inventions: British Photography in the 1980s (exh. cat.), British Council, London. Text by Ian Jeffrey.
Milena Kalinovska and Greg Hilty, *Richard Wentworth* (exh. cat.), Riverside Studios, London.

1988   *Richard Wentworth: Colección Imagen* (exh. cat.), Sala Parpalló, Valencia. Interview with Paul Bonaventura, introduction by Juan Vincente Aliaga.

1989   *British Object Sculptors of the '80s, I*, Art Random, ed. Marco Livingstone, Kyoto.
Richard Wentworth, Grenville Davey, Gerard Williams (exh. cat.), Sala 1, Rome. Text by Lynne Cooke.

1990   *Biennale of Sydney* (exh. cat.), Sydney.
Glasgow's Great British Art Exhibition (exh. cat.), Glasgow Museums and Art Galleries.
The New Urban Landscape (exh. cat.), Olympia & York Companies, New York. Ed. Richard Martin with texts by Richard Martin and Nancy Princenthal.

1991   *Objects for the Ideal Home: The Legacy of Pop Art* (exh. cat.), Serpentine Gallery, London.

1992	*Richard Wentworth* (exh. cat.), Kohji Ogura Gallery, Nagoya, Japan. Text by Jonathan Watkins.
1993	*The Saatchi Gift* (exh. cat.), Tate Gallery, London.
	British Sculpture from the Arts Council Collection (exh. cat.), Arts Council of Great Britain, London. Text by Greg Hilty.

FILMS

1985	*Making Do and Getting By*, video from Tapeslide, Whitechapel Art Gallery, London
1988	*Five British Sculptors*, director Julia Cave, BBC
	Richard Wentworth, video, Metronóm, Barcelona
1989	*Decoy*, director Mark James, video, Lisson Gallery, London
1991	*After Modernism: The Dilemma of Influence*, director Michael Blackwood, Michael Blackwood Productions in association with WDR/YLE

Richard Wentworth
Serpentine Gallery
6 November 1993 – 4 January 1994

Exhibition curated by Andrea Schlieker

Exhibition tour
Arnolfini, Bristol
19 January – 27 February 1994

Het Kruithuis
Municipal Museum for Contemporary Art
's-Hertogenbosh, The Netherlands
22 May – 3 July 1994

Musée des Beaux Arts et de la Dentelle, Calais
15 July – 30 September 1994

Serpentine Gallery staff

Director: Julia Peyton-Jones
Assistant Director: Andrea Schlieker
Administrator/Development: Rebecca King Lassman
Temporary Exhibition Organizer: Emma Anderson
Education: Vivien Ashley
Press and Publicity: Julia Little
Bookshop and Publications Managers: Gavin Everall and Ben Hillwood-Harris
Gallery Manager: Phil Monk
Gallery Accounts: Jackie McNerney
Secretary: Melanie Wilson
Gallery Assistants: Amanda Bracken, Michael Gaughan, Deborah Hursefield,
David Simpson, Paula Smithard

As an independent educational charity, the Serpentine Gallery gratefully
acknowledges the financial support it receives from the Arts Council of Great Britain
and Westminster City Council.

The Richard Wentworth exhibition has received financial support from The Henry
Moore Foundation and sponsorship from The Expanded Metal Company Ltd.

Registered charity no. 298890

The Serpentine Gallery
Kensington Gardens, London W2 3XA
Telephone 071 402 6075
Facsimile 071 402 4103